TABLE OF CONTENT

TABLE OF CONTENT 2
1. SPINACH AND POTATO PUREE 4
2. RASPBERRY COCONUT CHIA PUDDING 4
3. BUTTERNUT SQUASH AND PEAR PUREE 5
4. CREAMY SPINACH AND MUSHROOM DIP 6
5. BLUEBERRY BANANA PROTEIN SMOOTHIE 6
6. COMBINED BERRY CHIA PUDDING 7
7. CREAMY ASPARAGUS AND PEA SOUP 8
8. SOFT SCRAMBLED EGGS WITH SPINACH 9
9. CARROT AND GINGER MASH 10
10. SILKEN TOFU BERRY SMOOTHIE 10
11. CREAMY MUSHROOM AND THYME SOUP 11
12. CREAM OF LEEK AND POTATO SOUP 12
13. GREEK YOGURT AND HONEY PARFAIT 13
14. CHIA PUDDING WITH COMBINED BERRIES 13
15. CREAMY TOMATO AND BASIL BISQUE 14
16. CINNAMON APPLE OATMEAL 15
17. CREAMY ROASTED RED PEPPER SOUP 15
18. COCONUT MANGO SMOOTHIE 16
19. SWEET POTATO AND CAULIFLOWER PUREE 17
20. ROASTED BEETROOT HUMMUS 18
21. CREAMY MUSHROOM AND SPINACH RISOTTO 18
22. BLUEBERRY ALMOND PROTEIN SMOOTHIE 19
23. CREAM OF SPINACH SOUP 20
24. PUMPKIN AND BANANA SMOOTHIE 21
25. CREAMY BROCCOLI AND CAULIFLOWER SOUP 22
26. VANILLA BERRY CHIA PUDDING 23
27. SPINACH AND AVOCADO PUREE 23
28. CREAMY ROASTED GARLIC SOUP: 24
29. MANGO BANANA COCONUT SMOOTHIE: 25
30. SILKEN TOFU MANGO SMOOTHIE: 26

31. CREAMY CAULIFLOWER AND BROCCOLI SOUP: 26

32. PEVERY GREEK YOGURT PARFAIT 27

33. SOFT SCRAMBLED EGGS WITH HERBS 28

34. MASHED SWEET POTATOES WITH CINNAMON 28

35. CRANBERRY OATMEAL 29

36. RASPBERRY CHOCOLATE CHIA PUDDING: 30

37. BUTTERNUT SQUASH AND APPLE SOUP: 31

38. COMBINED FRUIT CHIA PUDDING: 31

39. TOMATO AND CARROT PUREE: 32

40. AVOCADO AND SPINACH DIP: 33

41. CREAMY LEEK AND POTATO SOUP: 33

42. PUMPKIN BANANA PROTEIN SMOOTHIE: 34

43. CREAMY ZUCCHINI AND SPINACH SOUP: 35

44. MANGO PINEAPPLE COCONUT SMOOTHIE: 36

45. APPLE CINNAMON CHIA PUDDING: 36

46. SPINACH AND BROCCOLI PUREE: 37

47. GREEK YOGURT AND COMBINED BERRY PARFAIT: 38

48. SOFT SCRAMBLED EGGS WITH CHEESE AND CHIVES: 39

49. CREAMY PEA AND MINT SOUP: 39

50. CREAMY ASPARAGUS AND POTATO SOUP 40

51. VANILLA RASPBERRY CHIA PUDDING 41

52. CREAM OF MUSHROOM SOUP 42

53. ROASTED RED PEPPER AND TOMATO PUREE 43

54. MASHED CAULIFLOWER AND CARROT 43

55. BLUEBERRY BANANA COCONUT SMOOTHIE 44

56. SILKEN TOFU BERRY BREAKFAST SMOOTHIE 45

57. CREAMY CARROT AND GINGER SOUP 45

58. SPINACH AND GREEN PEA PUREE...46

59. GREEK YOGURT AND ALMOND PARFAIT 47

60. SOFT SCRAMBLED EGGS WITH SMOKED SALMON: 47

61. CREAMY TOMATO AND RED PEPPER BISQUE: 48

62. BANANA PEANUT BUTTER PROTEIN SMOOTHIE: 49

1. SPINACH AND POTATO PUREE

Prep Time: 15 mins

Cook Time: 20 mins

Total Time: 35 mins

Servings: 4

Ingredients:
- 2 Big potatoes, peel off and diced
- 4 cups of fresh spinach leaves
- 1/2 cup of milk (dairy or plant-based)
- 2 tbsp butter or olive oil
- Salt and pepper as needed
- Finely grated nutmeg (non-compulsory)

Instructions:
1. In a pot of salted water, boil the diced potatoes up to they are fork-tender. Drain, then set apart.
2. Over medium heat, wilt the spinach in the same pot. Empty any extra water.
3. The cooked potatoes, wilted spinach, milk, butter or olive oil, salt, pepper, and a little amount of finely grated nutmeg, if using, Must all be combined in a blender or mixer.
4. If necessary, add more milk to change the consistency of the Mixture up to it is smooth and creamy.
5. If necessary, taste and adjust the seasoning.
6. If necessary, reheat the puree on the stove.
7. Warm potato and spinach puree Must be served.

Nutrition (per serving):

Cals: ~180, Protein: ~4g

Carbs: ~30g

Fat: ~6g, Fiber: ~4g

2. RASPBERRY COCONUT CHIA PUDDING

Prep Time: 10 mins

Cook Time: 0 mins

Total Time: 4 hrs 10 mins (including chilling time)

Servings: 2

Ingredients:
- 1/4 cup of chia seeds
- 1 cup of coconut milk

- 1/2 tsp vanilla extract
- 1 tbsp maple syrup (adjust as needed)
- 1/2 cup of fresh raspberries
- Shredded coconut, for garnish

Instructions:

1. Chia seeds, coconut milk, vanilla essence, and maple syrup Must all be combined in a bowl. Stir thoroughly.
2. Stir the Mixture once more to avoid clumping after letting it settle for 10 mins.
3. For at least 4 hrs or overnight, cover the bowl and place in the refrigerator.
4. Layer the chia pudding with fresh raspberries and coconut shreds before serving.
5. Cheers to the delicious and creamy chia pudding!

NUTRITION INFO (per serving):

Cals: ~250, Protein: 5g

Carbs: 24g

Fat: 16g, Fiber: 10g

3. BUTTERNUT SQUASH AND PEAR PUREE

Prep Time: 15 mins

Cook Time: 25 mins

Total Time: 40 mins

Servings: 4

Ingredients:

- 1 mini butternut squash, peel off, seeded, and diced
- 2 ripe pears, peel off, cored, and diced
- 1 tbsp olive oil
- 1/2 tsp ground cinnamon
- 1/4 tsp ground nutmeg
- Salt and pepper as needed
- 1/4 cup of water or vegetable broth

Instructions:

1. Olive oil Must be heated in a big skillet over a medium heat. Add the chop-up butternut squash and cook for 10 mins, or up to it begins to soften.
2. Pears diced, cinnamon, nutmeg, salt, and pepper Must be added. For a further 10-15 mins, sauté, or up to the squash and pears are soft.
3. Simmer for five more mins after adding water or veggie broth.
4. Blend the contents in a blender up to it is completely smooth.
5. The butternut squash and pear puree can be used as a side dish or as the foundation for other dishes.

NUTRITION INFO (per serving):

Cals: ~120, Protein: 1g

Carbs: 31g

Fat: 1g, Fiber: 6g

4. CREAMY SPINACH AND MUSHROOM DIP

Prep Time: 15 mins

Cook Time: 20 mins

Total Time: 35 mins

Servings: 6

Ingredients:
- 8 ozs fresh spinach, chop-up
- 8 ozs mushrooms, lightly chop-up
- 1 tbsp butter or olive oil
- 2 cloves garlic, chop-up
- 1/2 cup of cream cheese
- 1/4 cup of sour cream
- 1/4 cup of mayonnaise
- 1/4 cup of finely grated parmesan cheese
- Salt and pepper as needed

Instructions:
1. Melt butter or warm olive oil in a Big skillet over medium heat. Add the chop-up garlic and cook up to fragrant, about 1 min.
2. For 5-7 mins, or up to the mushrooms shed their moisture and turn golden, add the chop-up mushrooms.
3. Add the chop-up spinach and simmer for 3–4 mins, or up to wilted.
4. Cream cheese, sour cream, mayonnaise, and finely grated parmesan cheese Must be thoroughly combined in a bowl.
5. Combine the creamy Mixture and the sautéed vegetables. Add salt and pepper as needed.
6. Bake the Mixture at 375°F (190°C) for about 15 mins, or up to bubbling and golden on top. Transfer the Mixture to a baking dish.
7. Serve your preferred dippers alongside the creamy spinach and mushroom dip.

NUTRITION INFO (per serving):

Cals: ~150, Protein: 5g

Carbs: 4g

Fat: 14g, Fiber: 1g

5. BLUEBERRY BANANA PROTEIN SMOOTHIE

Prep Time: 5 mins

Cook Time: 0 mins

Total Time: 5 mins

Servings: 1

Ingredients:
- 1 ripe banana
- 1/2 cup of blueberries (fresh or refrigerated)
- 1 scoop vanilla protein powder
- 1/2 cup of Greek yogurt
- 1/2 cup of milk (dairy or plant-based)
- 1 tbsp almond butter or peanut butter (non-compulsory)
- Ice cubes

Instructions:
1. Blend the ripe banana, blueberries, protein powder, milk, Greek yogurt, and nut butter (if using) together in a blender.
2. Blend till creamy and smooth. Add more milk if the smoothie is too thick.
3. To freeze and thicken the smoothie, add ice cubes and blend one more.
4. Pour the protein smoothie with blueberries and bananas into a glass, and then savor it as a healthy breakfast or post-workout snack.

NUTRITION INFO (per serving):

Cals: ~350, Protein: 25g

Carbs: 45g

Fat: 10g, Fiber: 6g

6. COMBINED BERRY CHIA PUDDING

Prep Time: 10 mins

Cook Time: 0 mins

Total Time: 4 hrs 10 mins (includes chilling time)

Servings: 2

Ingredients:
- 1 cup of combined berries (strawberries, blueberries, raspberries)
- 1/4 cup of chia seeds
- 1 cup of almond milk (or any milk of your choice)
- 1 tbsp honey or maple syrup (adjust as needed)
- 1/2 tsp vanilla extract

Instructions:

1. To liberate their juices, crush half of the combined berries in a bowl with a fork.
2. To the mashed berries, add chia seeds, almond milk, honey or maple syrup, and vanilla extract. To blend, thoroughly stir.
3. Let the Mixture to rest for approximately 10 mins, stirring every so often to avoid clumping.
4. Give the Mixture one last swirl, cover the bowl, and chill for at least four hrs or overnight after the 10-min mark.
5. Give the pudding a good stir before serving. Divide it among serving glasses or bowls.
6. The remaining combined berries Must be added to the pudding.
7. Enjoy your chia pudding with combined berries!

Nutrition (per serving):

Cals: ~180, Protein: 4g

Carbs: 25g

Fat: 7g, Fiber: 10g

7. CREAMY ASPARAGUS AND PEA SOUP

Prep Time: 15 mins

Cook Time: 25 mins

Total Time: 40 mins

Servings: 4

Ingredients:

- 1 bunch asparagus, woody ends trimmed
- 1 cup of refrigerated peas
- 1 onion, chop-up
- 2 cloves garlic, chop-up
- 3 cups of vegetable broth
- 1 tbsp olive oil
- 1/2 cup of heavy cream or coconut cream
- Salt and pepper as needed
- Chop-up fresh parsley for garnish

Instructions:

1. Olive oil Must be heated in a sizable pot over medium heat. Add the chop-up garlic and onion, and cook up to transparent.
2. Along with the refrigerated peas, chop up the asparagus and put it to the pot. For a few mins, sauté.
3. Bring the Mixture to a boil after adding the veggie broth. For about 15-20 mins, or up to the vegetables are cooked, reduce the heat, cover, and simmer.
4. Up to the soup is creamy, purée it using an immersion blender. In the absence of an immersion blender, carefully transfer the soup in mini batches to a tabletop blender.

5. Reintroduce the pureed soup to the stove, then whisk in the heavy cream or coconut cream. As needed, add salt and pepper to the food.
6. Warm the soup completely over a low heat.
7. Serve the creamy asparagus and pea soup in dishes with fresh parsley that has been chop-up.

Nutrition (per serving):

Cals: ~220, Protein: 6g

Carbs: 18g

Fat: 15g, Fiber: 5g

8. SOFT SCRAMBLED EGGS WITH SPINACH

Prep Time: 5 mins

Cook Time: 5 mins

Total Time: 10 mins

Servings: 2

Ingredients:
- 4 Big eggs
- 1 cup of fresh spinach, chop-up
- Salt and pepper as needed
- 2 tbsp butter or olive oil
- Non-compulsory toppings: finely grated cheese, chop-up herbs

Instructions:
1. Crack the eggs into a bowl and beat them up to the whites and yolks are thoroughly combined. Add a little salt and pepper for seasoning.
2. Add the butter or olive oil to a nonstick skillet that is already heated to medium-low.
3. Add the chop-up spinach to the skillet once the butter has dilute or the oil is hot. Sauté the spinach for one to two mins, or up to it wilts.
4. In the skillet with the spinach, add the beaten eggs.
5. With a spatula, gently stir the egg and spinach combination, moving the Mixture from the sides to the middle of the skillet. As you cook, whisk the eggs occasionally up to they are softly set but still a little runny.
6. Just before the eggs are entirely cooked, turn off the heat source since they will continue to cook from the residual heat.
7. On plates, place the soft scrambled eggs and spinach. If desired, sprinkle with finely grated cheese and chop-up herbs.

Nutrition (per serving):

Cals: 220, Protein: 14g, Fat: 16g, Carbs: 3g

Fiber: 1g

9. CARROT AND GINGER MASH

Prep Time: 10 mins

Cook Time: 20 mins

Total Time: 30 mins

Servings: 4

Ingredients:

- 4 Big carrots, peel off and chop-up
- 1 tbsp fresh ginger, chop-up
- 2 tbsp butter
- Salt and pepper as needed
- 1/4 cup of milk or cream (non-compulsory)

Instructions:

1. Carrots Must be diced and added to a pot of boiling water. Cook the carrots for 15 to 20 mins, or up to they are fork-tender and soft.
2. The cooked carrots Must be drained and added to a combining dish.
3. To the bowl of cooked carrots, add the butter, salt, and pepper.
4. To achieve the appropriate consistency, mash the carrots using a fork or potato masher.
5. If you prefer a creamier texture, you can add milk or cream to the mashed carrots. Combine thoroughly.
6. If necessary, taste and adjust the seasoning.
7. The carrot and ginger mash Must be served as a side dish.

Nutrition (per serving, without milk/cream):

Cals: 90, Protein: 1g

Fat: 6g, Carbs: 9g, Fiber: 3g

10. SILKEN TOFU BERRY SMOOTHIE

Prep Time: 5 mins

Cook Time: 0 mins

Total Time: 5 mins

Servings: 2

Ingredients:

- 1 cup of combined berries (strawberries, blueberries, raspberries)
- 1/2 cup of silken tofu
- 1 banana
- 1/2 cup of almond milk (or any milk of your choice)

- 1 tbsp honey (non-compulsory)
- 1/2 tsp vanilla extract
- Ice cubes (non-compulsory)

Instructions:

1. The combined berries, silken tofu, banana, almond milk, honey (if used), and vanilla extract Must all be combined in a blender.
2. Blend till creamy and smooth. You can a little bit additional almond milk if the smoothie is too thick.
3. If desired, add ice cubes and reblend the smoothie up to it has the consistency you wish.
4. Serve the smoothie right away after pouring it into glasses.

Nutrition (per serving):

Cals: ~150, Protein: 6g

Carbs: 25g

Fat: 3g, Fiber: 4g

11. CREAMY MUSHROOM AND THYME SOUP

Prep Time: 10 mins

Cook Time: 25 mins

Total Time: 35 mins

Servings: 4

Ingredients:

- 1 lb mushrooms, split
- 1 onion, chop-up
- 3 cloves garlic, chop-up
- 2 tbsp butter or oil
- 4 cups of vegetable broth
- 1 tsp dried thyme
- 1/2 cup of heavy cream
- Salt and pepper as needed
- Fresh thyme leaves for garnish

Instructions:

1. Butter or oil Must be heated over medium heat in a big pot. Cook the chop-up onion up to transparent after adding it.
2. the split mushrooms and garlic, chop-up. Cook the mushrooms up to they are browned and the liquid has completely gone.
3. Add the dried thyme and then pour in the vegetable broth. After bringing to a simmer, cook for about 15 mins.
4. Up to the soup is creamy, purée it using an immersion blender. As an alternative, you may transfer the soup in stages to a blender, puree it up to smooth, and then return it to the saucepan.
5. Add the heavy cream, then simmer the soup for an additional five mins.

6. As needed, add salt and pepper to the food.
7. With fresh thyme leaves as a garnish, serve the soup hot.

Nutrition (per serving):

Cals: ~180, Protein: 4g

Carbs: 10g

Fat: 14g, Fiber: 2g

12. CREAM OF LEEK AND POTATO SOUP

Prep Time: 15 mins

Cook Time: 25 mins

Total Time: 40 mins

Servings: 6

Ingredients:
- 3 leeks, white and light green parts, cleaned and chop-up
- 3 potatoes, peel off and diced
- 1 onion, chop-up
- 3 tbsp butter
- 4 cups of vegetable broth
- 1 cup of milk (any type)
- Salt and pepper as needed
- Chop-up chives for garnish (non-compulsory)

Instructions:
1. Melt the butter in a Big pot over medium heat. Potatoes, onion, and leeks Must all be slice. Cook the vegetables up to they are tender but not browned.
2. Add the veggie broth, then boil the Mixture. For 20 to 25 mins, or up to the potatoes are soft, let it cook.
3. The soup Must be smooth and creamy after being blended with an immersion blender.
4. Add the milk, then whisk everything together. Simmer for a further five mins.
5. As needed, add salt and pepper to the food.
6. If preferred, top the heated soup with chop-up chives before serving.

Nutrition (per serving):

Cals: ~220, Protein: 5g

Carbs: 35g

Fat: 8g, Fiber: 4g

13. GREEK YOGURT AND HONEY PARFAIT

Prep Time: 10 mins

Cook Time: 0 mins

Total Time: 10 mins

Servings: 2

Ingredients:
- 1 cup of Greek yogurt
- 2 tbsp honey
- 1/2 cup of granola
- 1/2 cup of combined berries (strawberries, blueberries, raspberries)
- 2 tbsp chop-up nuts (almonds, walnuts, or your choice)

Instructions:
1. Start by adding a spoonful of Greek yogurt to the bottom of serving glasses or bowls.
2. Spread some honey on top of the yogurt layer.
3. After placing the yogurt and honey, sprinkle some granola over top.
4. Layer on some combined berries.
5. The layers are repeated up to the glasses are full, and then a drizzle of honey is added on top.
6. For extra crunch, scatter chop-up nuts over the top layer.
7. The parfaits can be served right away or stored in the fridge up to required.

Nutrition (per serving):

Cals: ~300, Protein: 15g, Carbs: 40g

Fat: 10g, Fiber: 4g

14. CHIA PUDDING WITH COMBINED BERRIES

Prep Time: 5 mins

Cook Time: 0 mins

Total Time: 4-8 hrs (including chilling time)

Servings: 2

Ingredients:
- 1/4 cup of chia seeds
- 1 cup of milk (dairy or plant-based)
- 1 tbsp honey or maple syrup
- 1/2 tsp vanilla extract
- 1/2 cup of combined berries (strawberries, blueberries, raspberries)

Instructions:

1. Chia seeds, milk, honey (or maple syrup), and vanilla essence Must all be combined in a bowl.
2. To prevent the chia seeds from clumping together, thoroughly stir the Mixture to spread them evenly.
3. For at least 4 hrs or overnight, cover the bowl and place in the refrigerator. To avoid clumping after the first hr, stir.
4. Give the pudding a good stir before serving.
5. Individual serving bowls containing the chia pudding Must be garnished with a variety of berries.

NUTRITION INFO (per serving):

Cals: ~180, Protein: 5g, Fat: 8g

Carbs: 23g, Fiber: 10g

15. CREAMY TOMATO AND BASIL BISQUE

Prep Time: 10 mins

Cook Time: 25 mins

Total Time: 35 mins

Servings: 4

Ingredients:

- 2 cans (28 oz every) whole tomatoes
- 1 mini onion, chop-up
- 3 cloves garlic, chop-up
- 2 cups of vegetable broth
- 1/2 cup of heavy cream
- 1/4 cup of fresh basil leaves, chop-up
- Salt and pepper as needed
- 2 tbsp olive oil

Instructions:

1. Olive oil is heated over medium heat in a big pot. Add the chop-up onion and cook it up to it is transparent.
2. Sauté for one more min after adding the chop-up garlic.
3. Add the vegetable broth together with the canned tomatoes and their juices. 20 mins Must pass after bringing to a simmer.
4. Up to the soup is creamy, purée it using an immersion blender. To puree the soup in batches if you don't have an immersion blender, carefully transfer the soup to a blender.
5. Add the heavy cream and chop-up basil to the soup before bringing it back to a simmer. Add salt and pepper as needed.
6. Warm the soup completely over a low heat.
7. If preferred, top the hot tomato and basil bisque with extra fresh basil.

NUTRITION INFO (per serving):

Cals: ~220, Protein: 4g

Fat: 14g, Carbs: 20g, Fiber: 4g

16. CINNAMON APPLE OATMEAL

Prep Time: 5 mins

Cook Time: 10 mins

Total Time: 15 mins

Servings: 2

Ingredients:
- 1 cup of rolled oats
- 2 cups of water or milk (dairy or plant-based)
- 1 apple, peel off, cored, and diced
- 1 tsp ground cinnamon
- 2 tbsp maple syrup or honey
- 1/4 cup of chop-up nuts (such as almonds or walnuts)
- Pinch of salt

Instructions:
1. Bring the milk or water to a medium boil in a saucepan.
2. Add the rolled oats and a dash of salt after stirring. Cook, stirring regularly, for about 5-7 mins, or up to the oats are cooked and the Mixture thickens, on medium-low heat.
3. Add the ground cinnamon and apple dice. Cook the apple for a further 2 to 3 mins, or up to it is soft.
4. Stir in the honey or maple syrup after taking the pan from the heat.
5. Oatmeal Must be served in bowls with chop-up nuts and additional cinnamon if preferred.

Nutrition (per serving):

Cals: ~300, Protein: 8g

Carbs: 55g

Fat: 7g, Fiber: 7g

17. CREAMY ROASTED RED PEPPER SOUP

Prep Time: 15 mins

Cook Time: 30 mins

Total Time: 45 mins

Servings: 4

Ingredients:

- 3 red bell peppers, roasted, peel off, and chop-up
- 1 onion, chop-up
- 2 cloves garlic, chop-up
- 3 cups of vegetable broth
- 1 can (14 oz) diced tomatoes
- 1/2 cup of heavy cream or coconut cream
- 1 tsp paprika
- Salt and pepper as needed
- Olive oil for cooking

Instructions:

1. Olive oil is heated in a big pot over medium heat. Add the chop-up garlic and onion. Sauté the onion up to it turns translucent.
2. Add the paprika, chop-up tomatoes with liquids, roasted red peppers, salt, and pepper. Let the flavors to mingle for about 10 mins as you cook.
3. Blend the Mixture with an immersion blender or in a standard blender up to it is completely smooth.
4. Refill the pot with the combined Mixture. Add the vegetable broth and boil while stirring.
5. Stir in the heavy cream or coconut cream after turning the heat down to low. For a another 5–10 mins, simmer.
6. If necessary, taste and adjust the seasoning. Offer the soup hot.

Nutrition (per serving):

Cals: ~180, Protein: 3g

Carbs: 18g

Fat: 12g, Fiber: 4g

18. COCONUT MANGO SMOOTHIE

Prep Time: 5 mins

Cook Time: 0 mins

Total Time: 5 mins

Servings: 2

Ingredients:

- 1 Big mango, peel off, pitted, and chop-up
- 1 banana, peel off and split
- 1 cup of coconut milk (from a can)
- 1/2 cup of Greek yogurt
- 1 tbsp honey or agave syrup
- 1/2 tsp vanilla extract
- Ice cubes (non-compulsory)

Instructions:

1. Blend together the chop-up mango, banana, Greek yogurt, honey, and vanilla essence with the coconut milk.
2. Blend the Mixture on high up to it is smooth and creamy. To chill the smoothie, if required, add a few ice cubes and combine once more.
3. Taste and, if necessary, add additional honey or agave to balance sweetness.
4. Serve the smoothie right away after pouring it into glasses.

Nutrition (per serving):

Cals: ~250, Protein: 5g

Carbs: 45g

Fat: 8g, Fiber: 4g

19. SWEET POTATO AND CAULIFLOWER PUREE

Prep Time: 10 mins

Cook Time: 25 mins

Total Time: 35 mins

Servings: 4

Ingredients:
- 2 sweet potatoes, peel off and cubed
- 1 mini head cauliflower, chop-up
- 2 cloves garlic, chop-up
- 2 tbsp butter or olive oil
- 1/4 cup of milk (dairy or plant-based)
- Salt and pepper as needed
- Chop-up fresh herbs (such as parsley or chives) for garnish

Instructions:
1. Bring water to a boil in a big pot. Add the chop-up cauliflower and sweet potato cubes. Boil for 15 to 20 mins, or up to both are tender.
2. Sweet potatoes and cauliflower Must be drained and added back to the stew.
3. Add milk, butter, or olive oil, along with the chop-up garlic, to the pot. To mash or combine ingredients up to smooth, use a potato masher or immersion blender.
4. As needed, add salt and pepper to the food. You can add a little more milk and combine if the puree is too thick.
5. If necessary, gently reheat the puree on the stove. Serve hot with freshly chop-up herbs as a garnish.

Nutrition (per serving):

Cals: ~150, Protein: 3g

Carbs: 30g

Fat: 4g, Fiber: 5g

20. ROASTED BEETROOT HUMMUS

Prep Time: 15 mins

Cook Time: 45 mins

Total Time: 1 hr

Servings: 6

Ingredients:

- 2 medium beetroots, peel off and cubed
- 1 can (15 oz) chickpeas, drained and rinsed
- 3 cloves garlic, chop-up
- 1/4 cup of tahini
- 1/4 cup of fresh lemon juice
- 3 tbsp olive oil
- 1 tsp ground cumin
- Salt and pepper as needed
- Water (as needed)
- Non-compulsory toppings: sesame seeds, chop-up parsley

Instructions:

1. Set the oven's temperature to 400°F (200°C).
2. Spread the cubed beets out on a baking sheet and toss them with a sprinkle of olive oil. Roast up to soft, about 45 mins.
3. Roasted beets, chickpeas, garlic, tahini, lemon juice, olive oil, ground cumin, salt, and pepper Must all be combined in a mixer.
4. Blend the contents in a mixer. If it's too thick, add a tbsp of water at a time up to you have the right consistency.
5. If necessary, taste and adjust the seasoning.
6. Place the hummus in a serving bowl and, if preferred, top with sesame seeds and parsley that has been lightly chop-up.
7. Serve alongside crackers, vegetable sticks, or pita bread.

Nutrition (per serving):

Cals: 180, Protein: 6g, Carbs: 17g, Fat: 11g

Fiber: 4g

21. CREAMY MUSHROOM AND SPINACH RISOTTO

Prep Time: 10 mins

Cook Time: 30 mins

Total Time: 40 mins

Servings: 4

Ingredients:

- 1 cup of Arborio rice
- 1/2 cup of white wine (non-compulsory)
- 4 cups of vegetable broth
- 1 tbsp olive oil
- 1 onion, lightly chop-up
- 2 cloves garlic, chop-up
- 8 oz mushrooms, split
- 2 cups of fresh spinach
- 1/4 cup of finely grated Parmesan cheese
- 2 tbsp butter
- Salt and pepper as needed
- Chop-up fresh parsley for garnish

Instructions:

1. The vegetable broth Must be warmed up in a saucepan over low heat.
2. Olive oil Must be heated in a big skillet over a medium heat. Sauté the onions till transparent after adding them.
3. the split mushrooms and garlic, chop-up. Cook the mushrooms up to they are well-browned and tender.
4. When the rice is just beginning to toast, add the Arborio and simmer, stirring regularly, for about 2 mins.
5. Wine Must be added to the skillet and cooked up to mostly absorbed.
6. One ladle at a time, start to add the warm vegetable broth; stir regularly and wait up to the liquid has been absorbed before adding more. Keep doing this up to the rice is creamy and al dente.
7. Add butter, freshly finely grated Parmesan cheese, and fresh spinach by stirring. Cook up to the cheese and butter are dilute and the spinach wilts.
8. Add salt and pepper to the risotto to suit your taste.
9. Serve the risotto hot with freshly chop-up parsley as a garnish.

Nutrition (per serving):

Cals: 320, Protein: 8g, Carbs: 45g

Fat: 10g, Fiber: 3g

22. BLUEBERRY ALMOND PROTEIN SMOOTHIE

Prep Time: 5 mins

Cook Time: 0 mins

Total Time: 5 mins

Servings: 2

Ingredients:

- 1 cup of refrigerated blueberries
- 1 banana
- 1 scoop vanilla protein powder
- 2 tbsp almond butter
- 1 cup of almond milk (or milk of your choice)
- 1/2 cup of Greek yogurt
- Honey or maple syrup as needed (non-compulsory)
- Ice cubes (non-compulsory)

Instructions:

1. Blend together the Greek yogurt, banana, protein powder, almond milk, and refrigerated blueberries.
2. Blend till creamy and smooth. You can adjust the smoothie's consistency by adding extra water or almond milk if it is too thick.
3. If you want the smoothie to be sweeter, add honey or maple syrup after tasting it.
4. To make the smoothie colder, if required, add ice cubes and blend once more.
5. Drink the smoothie right away after pouring it into glasses.

Nutrition (per serving):

Cals: 280, Protein: 15g

Carbs: 34g

Fat: 10g, Fiber: 6g

23. CREAM OF SPINACH SOUP

Prep Time: 10 mins

Cook Time: 20 mins

Total Time: 30 mins

Servings: 4

Ingredients:

- 1 tbsp butter
- 1 onion, chop-up
- 2 cloves garlic, chop-up
- 4 cups of fresh spinach, washed and chop-up
- 2 cups of vegetable broth
- 1 cup of milk (or milk alternative)
- 2 tbsp all-purpose flour
- Salt and pepper as needed
- Pinch of nutriment (non-compulsory)

- Sour cream or Greek yogurt for garnish (non-compulsory)

Instructions:

1. Melt the butter in a Big pot over medium heat. When the onion is transparent, add it and continue to cook.
2. Once aromatic, add the chop-up garlic and simmer for one more min.
3. To make a roux, sift the flour over the onions and garlic and whisk. To get rid of the raw taste of the flour, cook for a couple of mins.
4. Vegetable broth Must be added gradually while being stirred to avoid lumps.
5. The spinach Must be added to the pot and leted to wilt into the liquid.
6. As the soup thickens, pour the milk in and keep stirring.
7. To purée the soup up to it is smooth, either use an immersion blender or transfer it to a standard blender. Blend hot liquids carefully and in batches if you're using a standard blender.
8. Put the soup back in the pot and, if required, gently reheat.
9. If preferred, season the soup with nutmeg, salt, and pepper.
10. If desired, top the hot cream of spinach soup with a dollop of sour cream or Greek yogurt.

Nutrition (per serving):

Cals: 140, Protein: 6g

Carbs: 18g

Fat: 6g, Fiber: 2g

24. PUMPKIN AND BANANA SMOOTHIE

Prep Time: 5 mins

Cook Time: 0 mins

Total Time: 5 mins

Servings: 2

Ingredients:

- 1 cup of canned pumpkin puree
- 1 ripe banana
- 1 cup of milk (dairy or plant-based)
- 1/2 tsp ground cinnamon
- 1/4 tsp ground nutmeg
- 1 tbsp honey or maple syrup
- 1/2 cup of ice cubes

Instructions:

1. Blend the milk, ripe banana, pumpkin puree, cinnamon, nutmeg, and honey (or maple syrup) together in a blender.
2. Ice cubes Must be added to the combiner.
3. Blend the Mixture on high up to it is smooth and creamy.
4. If necessary, taste and adjust the sweetness or spices.

5. Pour into glasses and start serving right away.

NUTRITION INFO (per serving):

Cals: ~150, Protein: 3g

Carbs: 32g

Fat: 1g, Fiber: 5g

25. CREAMY BROCCOLI AND CAULIFLOWER SOUP

Prep Time: 10 mins

Cook Time: 25 mins

Total Time: 35 mins

Servings: 4

Ingredients:
- 1 tbsp olive oil
- 1 onion, chop-up
- 2 cloves garlic, chop-up
- 3 cups of broccoli florets
- 2 cups of cauliflower florets
- 4 cups of vegetable broth
- 1 cup of milk (dairy or plant-based)
- Salt and pepper as needed
- 1/4 cup of finely grated cheddar cheese (non-compulsory)
- Fresh parsley for garnish

Instructions:
1. Olive oil Must be heated in a sizable pot over medium heat. Add the chop-up garlic and onion, both chop-up. Sauté the onion up to it turns translucent.
2. Fill the pot with the broccoli and cauliflower florets. For a few mins, sauté.
3. The veggie broth Must be added and brought to a boil. When the vegetables are ready, turn the heat down, cover the pot, and simmer for about 15-20 mins.
4. Up to the soup is creamy, purée it using an immersion blender. Alternately, carefully add the soup in batches to a blender and process up to smooth. When using hot liquids in a blender, be careful.
5. Add the milk and then put the soup back in the pot. As needed, add salt and pepper to the food.
6. If using, add the finely grated cheddar cheese and combine up to it is dilute and smooth.
7. Serve the soup in dishes with fresh parsley as a garnish.

NUTRITION INFO (per serving, without cheese):

Cals: ~120, Protein: 6g

Carbs: 18g

Fat: 4g, Fiber: 5g

26. VANILLA BERRY CHIA PUDDING

Prep Time: 5 mins

Cook Time: 0 mins

Total Time: 4-6 hrs (or overnight)

Servings: 2

Ingredients:
- 1/4 cup of chia seeds
- 1 cup of milk (dairy or plant-based)
- 1 tsp vanilla extract
- 1 tbsp honey or maple syrup (adjust as needed)
- Assorted berries for topping (e.g., strawberries, blueberries, raspberries)

Instructions:
1. Combine the chia seeds, milk, vanilla essence, honey, and/or maple syrup in a bowl.
2. To ensure that the chia seeds are completely submerged in the liquid, stir thoroughly.
3. For at least 4-6 hrs or overnight, cover the bowl and place in the refrigerator. Chia seeds will thicken the Mixture by absorbing the liquid.
4. Give the chia pudding a quick toss just before serving to take out any clumps and ensure a smooth texture.
5. Place selected berries on top of the chia pudding after dividing it among serving glasses.
6. Offer cold.

NUTRITION INFO (per serving):

Cals: ~180, Protein: 5g

Carbs: 20g

Fat: 9g, Fiber: 10g

27. SPINACH AND AVOCADO PUREE

Prep Time: 5 mins

Cook Time: 0 mins

Total Time: 5 mins

Servings: 2

Ingredients:

- 2 cups of fresh spinach leaves
- 1 ripe avocado, peel off and pitted
- 1 clove garlic, chop-up
- 2 tbsp lemon juice
- 2 tbsp olive oil
- Salt and pepper as needed
- Red pepper flakes for a hint of spice (non-compulsory)

Instructions:

1. Combine the fresh spinach, ripe avocado, chop-up garlic, lemon juice, and olive oil in a mixer or blender.
2. Blend till creamy and smooth.
3. To further meld the flavors, season with salt, pepper, and red pepper flakes (if using).
4. If necessary, taste and adjust the seasoning.
5. Put the purée in dishes for serving.
6. This puree can be used as a spread, a sauce for pasta or vegetables, or even as a dip.

NUTRITION INFO (per serving):

Cals: ~160, Protein: 2g

Carbs: 7g

Fat: 15g, Fiber: 5g

28. CREAMY ROASTED GARLIC SOUP:

Prep Time: 15 mins

Cook Time: 1 hr

Total Time: 1 hr 15 mins

Servings: 4

Ingredients:

- 2 heads of garlic
- 1 tbsp olive oil
- 1 onion, chop-up
- 3 cups of vegetable broth
- 2 medium potatoes, peel off and diced
- 1 tsp thyme
- 1 bay leaf
- 1 cup of heavy cream
- Salt and pepper as needed
- Chop-up chives (for garnish)

Instructions:

1. Set the oven's temperature to 400°F (200°C).

2. Take out the garlic heads' tops to reveal the cloves. They Must be placed on a sheet of aluminum foil, covered with olive oil, and then securely wrapped. The garlic cloves Must be roasted in the preheated oven for about 40 mins, or up to they are tender.
3. The chop-up onion Must be cooked up to transparent in a big pot.
4. Add the diced potatoes, thyme, and bay leaf to the saucepan along with the squeezed roasted garlic cloves. Cook for a little while.
5. The veggie broth Must be added and brought to a boil. Turn down the heat, cover, and cook the potatoes for a while.
6. Use an immersion blender to purée the soup up to it is smooth after removing the bay leaf.
7. The heavy cream is then added, and the soup is gradually heated. Add salt and pepper as needed.
8. Serve hot with chop-up chives as a garnish.

NUTRITION INFO (per serving):

Cals: 280, Fat: 18g, Carbs: 25g

Protein: 5g, Fiber: 3g

29. MANGO BANANA COCONUT SMOOTHIE:

Prep Time: 5 mins

Cook Time: 0 mins

Total Time: 5 mins

Servings: 2

Ingredients:
- 1 ripe mango, peel off and pitted
- 1 ripe banana
- 1/2 cup of coconut milk
- 1/2 cup of plain yogurt
- 1 tbsp honey (non-compulsory)
- Ice cubes

Instructions:
1. Mango and banana Must be chop-up up.
2. Mango chunks, banana, coconut milk, yogurt, and honey (if using) Must all be combined in a blender.
3. Blend till creamy and smooth.
4. If desired, add ice cubes and blend one more to chill the smoothie.
5. Pour into glasses and start serving right away.

NUTRITION INFO (per serving):

Cals: 180, Fat: 6g

Carbs: 31g

Protein: 3g, Fiber: 3g

30. SILKEN TOFU MANGO SMOOTHIE:

Prep Time: 5 mins

Cook Time: 0 mins

Total Time: 5 mins

Servings: 2

Ingredients:
- 1 cup of ripe mango chunks
- 1/2 cup of silken tofu
- 1/2 cup of orange juice
- 1/2 cup of almond milk
- 1 tbsp honey or maple syrup
- 1/2 tsp vanilla extract
- Ice cubes

Instructions:
1. In a blender, combine the orange juice, mango chunks, silken tofu, almond milk, honey, maple syrup, and vanilla extract.
2. Blend the Mixture up to it's creamy and smooth.
3. If desired, add ice cubes and blend one more to chill the smoothie.
4. Pour into glasses, then offer.

NUTRITION INFO (per serving):

Cals: 150, Fat: 2.5g, Carbs: 29g

Protein: 4g, Fiber: 2g

31. CREAMY CAULIFLOWER AND BROCCOLI SOUP:

Prep Time: 10 mins

Cook Time: 30 mins

Total Time: 40 mins

Servings: 6

Ingredients:
- 1 medium cauliflower, florets separated
- 1 broccoli crown, florets separated
- 1 onion, chop-up
- 2 cloves garlic, chop-up
- 4 cups of vegetable broth
- 1 cup of milk (or non-dairy milk)

- 2 tbsp butter (or olive oil for vegan)
- Salt and pepper as needed
- Chop-up fresh parsley (for garnish)

Instructions:

1. Melt the butter in a Big pot over medium heat. Add the chop-up garlic and onion, both chop-up. Sauté the onion up to it turns translucent.
2. Broccoli and cauliflower florets can be added to the stew. The veggie broth Must be added and brought to a boil. Till the vegetables are cooked, lower the heat and let it simmer.
3. Up to the soup is creamy, purée it using an immersion blender.
4. Add the milk, then slowly reheat the soup. Add salt and pepper as needed.
5. Serve hot with freshly chop-up parsley as a garnish.

NUTRITION INFO (per serving):

Cals: 120, Fat: 5g

Carbs: 15g

Protein: 5g, Fiber: 5g

32. PEVERY GREEK YOGURT PARFAIT

Prep Time: 10 mins

Cook Time: 0 mins

Total Time: 10 mins

Servings: 2

Ingredients:

- 1 cup of Greek yogurt
- 1 cup of diced peaches (fresh or canned)
- 1/2 cup of granola
- 2 tbsp honey
- 1/4 tsp vanilla extract

Instructions:

1. The Greek yogurt Must be layered in half in serving glasses or bowls.
2. On top of the yogurt, scatter half of the diced peaches.
3. Granola is strewn on top of the peaches.
4. Give the granola a tbsp of honey to drizzle on top.
5. With the remaining ingredients, repeat the layers.
6. Add vanilla extract and a drizzle of honey on the top to complete the dish.
7. Serve right away and delight in!

NUTRITION INFO (per serving):

Cals: ~300, Protein: 15g, Carbs: 45g

Fat: 8g, Fiber: 4g

33. SOFT SCRAMBLED EGGS WITH HERBS

Prep Time: 5 mins

Cook Time: 5 mins

Total Time: 10 mins

Servings: 2

Ingredients:
- 4 Big eggs
- 2 tbsp milk
- Salt and pepper as needed
- 2 tbsp chop-up fresh herbs (such as chives, parsley, or dill)
- 1 tbsp butter

Instructions:
1. In a bowl, crack the eggs, add the milk, and whisk to combine. Add salt and pepper as needed.
2. In a nonstick skillet, melt the butter over medium-low heat.
3. After pouring the egg Mixture into the skillet, wait a short while before moving on.
4. With a spatula, gently whisk the eggs, moving them from the edges to the middle.
5. The eggs Must continue to cook and gently whisk up to they are just barely set but not quite set.
6. Take the skillet from the stove. The eggs will continue to be cooked to perfection by the residual heat.
7. Give the scrambled eggs one more gentle toss before scattering the chop-up herbs on top.
8. Serve right away with toast or your preferred side dishes.

NUTRITION INFO (per serving):

Cals: ~180, Protein: 13g

Carbs: 2g

Fat: 13g, Fiber: 0g

34. MASHED SWEET POTATOES WITH CINNAMON

Prep Time: 10 mins

Cook Time: 20 mins

Total Time: 30 mins

Servings: 4

Ingredients:
- 2 Big sweet potatoes, peel off and cubed
- 2 tbsp butter
- 1/4 cup of milk (or as needed)
- 1 tsp ground cinnamon
- Salt as needed

Instructions:
1. Put the sweet potato cubes in a pot and add water to cover them. Put a dash of salt in.
2. Sweet potatoes Must be cooked in boiling water for 15 to 20 mins, or up to they can easily be punctured with a fork.
3. Sweet potatoes Must be drained and added back to the pot.
4. The sweet potatoes Must be combined with butter, cinnamon powder, and a little salt.
5. Use a potato masher or fork to mash the sweet potatoes up to they are smooth and creamy. When necessary, add milk to achieve the desired consistency.
6. If necessary, add more salt or cinnamon after tasting the dish to suit your tastes.
7. Warm mashed sweet potatoes are best served as a side dish.

NUTRITION INFO (per serving):

Cals: ~150, Protein: 2g

Carbs: 27g

Fat: 5g, Fiber: 4g

35. CRANBERRY OATMEAL

Prep Time: 5 mins

Cook Time: 10 mins

Total Time: 15 mins

Servings: 2

Ingredients:
- 1 cup of old-fashioned oats
- 2 cups of water or milk (dairy or plant-based)
- 1/2 cup of dried cranberries
- 2 tbsp honey or maple syrup
- 1/4 tsp vanilla extract
- Pinch of salt
- Non-compulsory toppings: chop-up nuts, additional dried cranberries

Instructions:
1. Bring the milk or water to a medium boil in a saucepan.
2. Turn the heat down to medium-low after stirring in the oats. Cook the oats for about 5-7 mins, stirring occasionally, or up to they are creamy and the proper consistency.

3. Add the honey, maple syrup, vanilla essence, and a dash of salt after stirring in the dried cranberries. additional 2 to 3 mins of cooking.
4. Oatmeal Must be taken off the heat and let to thicken for a min.
5. If preferred, add more dried cranberries and chop-up nuts to the top of every bowl of oats after dividing it into portions.
6. Warm cranberry oatmeal Must be served.

NUTRITION INFO (per serving):

Cals: ~300, Protein: 6g

Carbs: 65g

Fat: 3g, Fiber: 6g

36. RASPBERRY CHOCOLATE CHIA PUDDING:

Prep Time: 10 mins

Cook Time: 0 mins

Total Time: 4 hrs 10 mins (includes chilling time)

Servings: 2

Ingredients:
- 1/4 cup of chia seeds
- 1 cup of almond milk (or any milk of your choice)
- 2 tbsp cocoa powder
- 1 tbsp maple syrup (adjust as needed)
- 1/2 tsp vanilla extract
- 1/2 cup of raspberries (fresh or refrigerated)
- Dark chocolate shavings for garnish

Instructions:
1. Chia seeds, almond milk, chocolate powder, maple syrup, and vanilla extract Must all be combined in a bowl.
2. Let the Mixture to rest for approximately 10 mins, and then whisk it once more to avoid clumping.
3. For at least 4 hrs or overnight, cover the bowl and place in the refrigerator.
4. To make a raspberry sauce before serving, puree half of the raspberries.
5. In serving glasses, stack the chia pudding and raspberry sauce to assemble. Add the remaining raspberries and shavings of dark chocolate on top.
6. The raspberry chocolate chia pudding is delicious!

Nutrition (per serving):

Cals: 220, Protein: 5g, Carbs: 28g

Fat: 10g, Fiber: 12g

37. BUTTERNUT SQUASH AND APPLE SOUP:

Prep Time: 15 mins

Cook Time: 35 mins

Total Time: 50 mins

Servings: 4

Ingredients:
- 1 medium butternut squash, peel off, seeded, and cubed
- 2 apples, peel off, cored, and chop-up
- 1 onion, chop-up
- 2 cloves garlic, chop-up
- 4 cups of vegetable broth
- 1 tsp ground cinnamon
- 1/2 tsp ground nutmeg
- Salt and pepper as needed
- 2 tbsp olive oil
- 1/4 cup of heavy cream (non-compulsory, for creaminess)
- Chop-up fresh parsley for garnish

Instructions:
1. Olive oil Must be heated in a sizable pot over medium heat. Add the chop-up garlic and onion, and cook up to melted.
2. Add the apple and butternut squash cubes. For a few mins, sauté.
3. Pour in the veggie broth and season with salt, pepper, cinnamon, and nutmeg. When the squash and apples are soft, turn down the heat, cover, and simmer for about 25 to 30 mins.
4. Up to the soup is creamy, purée it using an immersion blender. Let the soup to cool somewhat before combining it in portions if using a conventional blender.
5. For more creaminess, if desired, combine in the heavy cream.
6. If required, reheat the soup and serve it hot. Add chop-up parsley as a garnish.

Nutrition (per serving):

Cals: 220, Protein: 3g, Carbs: 40g

Fat: 7g, Fiber: 8g

38. COMBINED FRUIT CHIA PUDDING:

Prep Time: 10 mins

Total Time: 4 hrs (including chilling time)

Servings: 2

Ingredients:

- 1/4 cup of chia seeds
- 1 cup of almond milk (or any milk of your choice)
- 1 tbsp honey or maple syrup
- 1/2 tsp vanilla extract
- Combined fruits (such as berries, kiwi, mango), chop-up

Instructions:

1. Chia seeds, almond milk, honey (or maple syrup), and vanilla essence Must all be combined in a bowl. To blend, thoroughly stir.
2. Let the Mixture to rest for approximately 10 mins, stirring every so often to avoid clumping.
3. For best results, leave the bowl in the fridge overnight, but at least for three to four hrs.
4. Give the chia pudding a thorough swirl just before serving. More almond milk can be added if the pudding is too thick.
5. In serving glasses or bowls, arrange the chia pudding and assorted fruits in layers.
6. Enjoy while serving chilled!

Nutrition (per serving):

Cals: ~220, Protein: 6g

Carbs: 30g

Fiber: 10g, Fat: 9g

39. TOMATO AND CARROT PUREE:

Prep Time: 15 mins

Cook Time: 25 mins

Total Time: 40 mins

Servings: 4

Ingredients:

- 4 Big tomatoes, quartered
- 4 Big carrots, peel off and chop-up
- 1 onion, chop-up
- 2 cloves garlic, chop-up
- 2 cups of vegetable broth
- 1 tbsp olive oil
- Salt and pepper as needed
- Fresh basil leaves for garnish

Instructions:

1. Olive oil is heated over medium heat in a big pot. Add the garlic and onions, and cook up to transparent.
2. Add diced tomatoes and carrots. Cook the vegetables for about 10 mins, or up to they soften.

3. Vegetable broth Must be added. Bring to a boil, then lower the heat and simmer for an additional fifteen mins.
4. Blend the Mixture with an immersion blender or in a standard blender up to it is completely smooth.
5. Add salt and pepper to the purée before adding it back to the saucepan to finish heating.
6. Serve hot with fresh basil leaves as a garnish.

Nutrition (per serving):

Cals: ~90, Protein: 2g

Carbs: 18g

Fiber: 4g, Fat: 2g

40. AVOCADO AND SPINACH DIP:

Prep Time: 10 mins

Total Time: 10 mins

Servings: 6

Ingredients:
- 2 ripe avocados, peel off and pitted
- 2 cups of fresh spinach leaves
- 1/4 cup of Greek yogurt
- 2 cloves garlic, chop-up
- 1 mini onion, chop-up
- 1 tbsp lemon juice
- Salt and pepper as needed

Instructions:
1. Avocados, spinach, Greek yogurt, garlic, onion, and lemon juice are all combined in a mixer.
2. The Mixture Must be pulsed up to it reaches the appropriate consistency.
3. As needed, add salt and pepper to the food.
4. Put the dip in a bowl for serving.
5. Serve with pita bread, veggie sticks, or tortilla chips.

Nutrition (per serving):

Cals: ~120, Protein: 3g

Carbs: 8g

Fiber: 5g, Fat: 9g

41. CREAMY LEEK AND POTATO SOUP:

Prep Time: 15 mins

Cook Time: 30 mins

Total Time: 45 mins

Servings: 4

Ingredients:

- 3 leeks, white and light green parts, cleaned and chop-up
- 3 Big potatoes, peel off and diced
- 1 onion, chop-up
- 2 cloves garlic, chop-up
- 4 cups of vegetable broth
- 1 cup of milk or heavy cream
- 2 tbsp butter
- Salt and pepper as needed
- Chop-up chives for garnish

Instructions:

1. Melt butter over medium heat in a big pot. Leeks, onions, and garlic Must be chop-up. up to melted, sauté.
2. Add veggie broth and cubed potatoes. The potatoes Must be cooked after 20 to 25 mins of simmering after bringing to a boil.
3. Blend the Mixture with an immersion blender or in a standard blender up to it is completely smooth.
4. Bring the soup back to a simmer in the same pot, add the milk or cream, and heat without boiling.
5. Add salt and pepper as needed.
6. Serve hot with chop-up chives as a garnish.

Nutrition (per serving):

Cals: ~250, Protein: 5g

Carbs: 35g

Fiber: 4g, Fat: 10g

42. PUMPKIN BANANA PROTEIN SMOOTHIE:

Prep Time: 5 mins

Cook Time: 0 mins

Total Time: 5 mins

Servings: 2

Ingredients:

- 1/2 cup of canned pumpkin puree
- 1 ripe banana
- 1 scoop vanilla protein powder
- 1 cup of almond milk
- 1/2 tsp pumpkin pie spice

- 1 tbsp honey or maple syrup (non-compulsory)
- Ice cubes

Instructions:
1. Pumpkin puree, a ripe banana, protein powder, almond milk, pumpkin pie spice, and honey or maple syrup (if used) Must all be put in a blender.
2. A few ice cubes Must be added to the combiner.
3. Blend till creamy and smooth.
4. Taste, and if necessary, adjust the amount of sweetness or spice.
5. Pour into glasses and start serving right away.

Nutrition (per serving):

Cals: ~180, Protein: ~15g

Carbs: ~25g, Fat: ~3g, Fiber: ~5g

43. CREAMY ZUCCHINI AND SPINACH SOUP:

Prep Time: 10 mins

Cook Time: 25 mins

Total Time: 35 mins

Servings: 4

Ingredients:
- 2 medium zucchinis, chop-up
- 3 cups of fresh spinach leaves
- 1 onion, chop-up
- 2 cloves garlic, chop-up
- 4 cups of vegetable broth
- 1 tbsp olive oil
- 1 tsp dried thyme
- Salt and pepper as needed
- 1/2 cup of coconut milk (non-compulsory)

Instructions:
1. Olive oil Must be heated in a sizable pot over medium heat. Add the chop-up garlic and onion, and cook up to transparent.
2. To the pot, add the diced zucchini and dry thyme. Cook the zucchini for a few mins, or up to they begin to soften.
3. The veggie broth Must be added and brought to a boil. Once the zucchinis are soft, turn down the heat and let it simmer for about 15 to 20 mins.
4. Add the spinach and stir up to it wilts.
5. To make the soup smooth and creamy, purée it using an immersion blender. If using coconut milk, do that now and combine once more.
6. As needed, add salt and pepper to the food.

7. Serve the hot soup garnished, at your discretion, with a drizzle of coconut milk and some dried thyme.

Nutrition (per serving without coconut milk):

Cals: ~90, Protein: ~3g

Carbs: ~12g

Fat: ~4g, Fiber: ~3g

44. MANGO PINEAPPLE COCONUT SMOOTHIE:

- Prep Time: 5 mins
- Cook Time: 0 mins
- Total Time: 5 mins
- Servings: 2

Ingredients:

- 1 ripe mango, peel off and diced
- 1 cup of diced pineapple
- 1/2 cup of coconut milk
- 1/2 cup of Greek yogurt
- 1 tbsp honey or agave syrup (non-compulsory)
- Ice cubes

Instructions:

1. Mango and pineapple dice, coconut milk, Greek yogurt, and honey or agave syrup (if using) Must all be combined in a blender.
2. A few ice cubes Must be added to the combiner.
3. Blend till creamy and smooth.
4. If necessary, taste and add additional sweetener.
5. Pour into glasses, then immediately indulge.

Nutrition (per serving):

Cals: ~200, Protein: ~4g

Carbs: ~40g

Fat: ~5g, Fiber: ~3g

45. APPLE CINNAMON CHIA PUDDING:

Prep Time: 10 mins (+ chilling time)

Cook Time: 0 mins

Total Time: 10 mins (+ chilling time)

Servings: 2

Ingredients:
- 1 cup of almond milk (or any milk of your choice)
- 1/4 cup of chia seeds
- 1 apple, finely grated or lightly chop-up
- 1 tsp honey or maple syrup
- 1/2 tsp ground cinnamon
- 1/4 tsp vanilla extract

Instructions:
1. Almond milk, chia seeds, honey or maple syrup, ground cinnamon, and vanilla extract Must all be combined in a bowl.
2. Stir well before adding the finely grated or chop-up apple to the Mixture.
3. For at least two hrs or overnight, cover the bowl and place in the fridge. As a result, the chia seeds can absorb the liquid and take on the consistency of pudding.
4. Give the pudding a good stir before serving. To get the right consistency, add a little more almond milk if it's too thick.
5. Pour the chia pudding into serving glasses and, if desired, top with more cinnamon.
6. Take pleasure in as a wholesome breakfast or snack.

Nutrition (per serving):
Cals: ~180, Protein: ~5g

Carbs: ~22g

Fat: ~8g, Fiber: ~9g

46. SPINACH AND BROCCOLI PUREE:

Prep Time: 10 mins

Cook Time: 15 mins

Total Time: 25 mins

Servings: 4

Ingredients:
- 2 cups of fresh spinach leaves, washed
- 1 cup of broccoli florets
- 1 mini onion, chop-up
- 2 cloves garlic, chop-up
- 1 tbsp olive oil
- 1 cup of vegetable broth
- Salt and pepper as needed

Instructions:
1. Olive oil Must be heated in a medium-sized pot over medium heat. Add the chop-up garlic and onion, both chop-up. Sauté the onion up to it turns translucent.

2. Broccoli florets and vegetable broth Must be added to the pot. Bring to a simmer and cook the broccoli for 8 to 10 mins, or up to it is cooked.
3. Fresh spinach leaves Must be added to the pot and cooked for a further two to three mins, or up to wilted.
4. Blend the Mixture very gently, either with an immersion blender or a standard blender, up to it is smooth. If using a standard blender, let the Mixture cool down a bit first.
5. As needed, add salt and pepper to the purée.
6. Warm spinach and broccoli puree can be used as a side dish or nutritious dip.

NUTRITION INFO (per serving):

Cals: 70, Protein: 3g

Carbs: 9g

Fat: 3g, Fiber: 3g

47. GREEK YOGURT AND COMBINED BERRY PARFAIT:

Prep Time: 10 mins

Total Time: 10 mins

Servings: 2

Ingredients:
- 1 cup of Greek yogurt
- 1 cup of combined berries (strawberries, blueberries, raspberries)
- 2 tbsp honey or maple syrup
- 1/4 cup of granola

Instructions:
1. Start by adding a spoonful of Greek yogurt to the bottom of serving glasses or bowls.
2. To the yogurt, add a layer of combined berries.
3. Over the fruit, drizzle some honey or maple syrup.
4. The layers are repeated up to the glasses are full, and then a layer of berries is placed on top to complete.
5. Over the top of the last layer of berries, scatter granola.
6. Serve right away for a delectable and wholesome breakfast or dessert.

NUTRITION INFO (per serving):

Cals: 220, Protein: 12g

Carbs: 40g

Fat: 2g, Fiber: 5g

48. SOFT SCRAMBLED EGGS WITH CHEESE AND CHIVES:

Prep Time: 5 mins

Cook Time: 5 mins

Total Time: 10 mins

Servings: 2

Ingredients:
- 4 Big eggs
- 1/4 cup of shredded cheddar cheese
- 2 tbsp chop-up chives
- Salt and pepper as needed
- 2 tbsp butter

Instructions:
1. In a bowl, crack the eggs, season with salt and pepper, and whisk to combine.
2. Melt the butter in a nonstick skillet over low heat.
3. The eggs Must start to set around the edges after being added to the skillet after being whisked.
4. With a spatula, gently whisk the eggs, moving them from the edges to the middle.
5. Till the eggs are softly set but still little creamy, continue to simmer and gently stir.
6. Over the eggs, scatter the cheddar cheese and stir up to it melts.
7. Add the chop-up chives after taking the pan off the heat.
8. Warm soft scrambled eggs may be served with bread or in any other way.

NUTRITION INFO (per serving):

Cals: 250, Protein: 18g

Carbs: 2g

Fat: 19g, Fiber: 0g

49. CREAMY PEA AND MINT SOUP:

Prep Time: 10 mins

Cook Time: 20 mins

Total Time: 30 mins

Servings: 4

Ingredients:
- 2 cups of refrigerated peas
- 1 mini onion, chop-up

- 2 cloves garlic, chop-up
- 4 cups of vegetable broth
- 1/2 cup of fresh mint leaves
- 1/2 cup of heavy cream
- Salt and pepper as needed
- Olive oil for sautéing

Instructions:

1. Olive oil is heated in a pot over medium heat. Add the chop-up garlic and onion, both chop-up. The onion Must be cooked up to tender and transparent.
2. Refrigerate peas and vegetable broth Must be added to the stew. After bringing to a boil, simmer for about ten mins.
3. Add the fresh mint leaves after turning off the stove.
4. Up to the soup is creamy, purée it using an immersion blender. If using a standard blender, let the soup cool a bit first, puree it, and then transfer the Mixture back to the pot.
5. Add the heavy cream and season as needed with salt and pepper. If necessary, gently reheat the soup.
6. Serve the hot, creamy pea and mint soup with a few more mint leaves as a garnish, if preferred.

NUTRITION INFO (per serving):

Cals: 180, Protein: 6g

Carbs: 18g

Fat: 10g, Fiber: 5g

50. CREAMY ASPARAGUS AND POTATO SOUP

Prep Time: 15 mins

Cook Time: 25 mins

Total Time: 40 mins

Servings: 4

Ingredients:

- 1 lb (450g) asparagus, trimmed and chop-up
- 2 medium potatoes, peel off and diced
- 1 onion, chop-up
- 2 cloves garlic, chop-up
- 4 cups of vegetable broth
- 1 cup of heavy cream
- Salt and pepper as needed
- 2 tbsp olive oil
- Fresh chop-up chives for garnish

Instructions:

1. Olive oil Must be heated in a sizable pot over medium heat. When the onion is transparent, add it and continue to cook.
2. Potato dice and garlic powder Must be added. Cook the potatoes for a few mins or up to they begin to soften.
3. The veggie broth Must be added and brought to a boil. Cook the potatoes at a simmering temperature up to they are fork-tender.
4. When the asparagus is cooked but still bright green, add the chop-up asparagus and simmer for an additional 5-7 mins.
5. Up to the soup is creamy, purée it using an immersion blender.
6. Add the heavy cream and season as needed with salt and pepper. After adding the cream, slowly reheat the soup, being careful not to let it boil.
7. Serve the soup hot with freshly chop-up chives as a garnish.

NUTRITION INFO (per serving):

Cals: 280, Fat: 18g

Carbs: 26g

Fiber: 4g, Protein: 5g

51. VANILLA RASPBERRY CHIA PUDDING

Prep Time: 10 mins

Total Time: 4 hrs (including chilling time)

Servings: 2

Ingredients:
- 1 cup of milk (dairy or plant-based)
- 1/4 cup of chia seeds
- 1 tbsp maple syrup or honey
- 1 tsp vanilla extract
- 1/2 cup of raspberries
- Split almonds for topping

Instructions:
1. Combine the milk, chia seeds, maple syrup, honey, and vanilla essence in a bowl.
2. Let the Mixture to rest for around 15 mins, stirring every so often to avoid clumps developing.
3. Cover the bowl after the first 15 mins and chill for at least 3 hrs or overnight. As a result, the chia seeds can absorb the liquid and take on the consistency of pudding.
4. Make sure the chia pudding is well blended and creamy before serving by giving it a good swirl.
5. Fresh raspberries and split almonds Must be added to the pudding before serving in individual glasses or bowls.

NUTRITION INFO (per serving):

Cals: 220, Fat: 9g

Carbs: 27g

Fiber: 14g, Protein: 7g

52. CREAM OF MUSHROOM SOUP

Prep Time: 15 mins

Cook Time: 25 mins

Total Time: 40 mins

Servings: 4

Ingredients:
- 1 lb (450g) mushrooms, split
- 1 medium onion, chop-up
- 2 cloves garlic, chop-up
- 3 tbsp butter
- 3 tbsp all-purpose flour
- 4 cups of vegetable or chicken broth
- 1 cup of heavy cream
- Salt and pepper as needed
- Fresh parsley, chop-up (for garnish)

Instructions:
1. Melt the butter in a Big pot over medium heat. Add the chop-up garlic and onion, both chop-up. Sauté the onion up to it turns translucent.
2. Split mushrooms Must be added and cooked up to they release moisture and turn brown.
3. The flour Must be added to the mushrooms and combined thoroughly. To get rid of the raw taste of the flour, cook for a couple of mins.
4. Pour the broth in gradually, continually stirring to prevent lumps. For 10 to 15 mins, let the soup boil.
5. Up to the soup is creamy, combine it using an immersion blender. As an alternative, carefully transfer the soup in batches to a blender to combine.
6. Refill the pot with the blended soup. After adding the heavy cream, boil the Mixture for a further five mins.
7. As desired, season the soup with salt and pepper.
8. Hot cream of mushroom soup Must be served with fresh parsley that has been chop-up on top.

Nutrition (per serving):
Cals: Approximately 280 kcal

Fat: 23g, Carbs: 15g

Fiber: 2g, Protein: 4g

53. ROASTED RED PEPPER AND TOMATO PUREE

Prep Time: 10 mins

Cook Time: 30 mins

Total Time: 40 mins

Servings: 6

Ingredients:
- 3 Big red bell peppers
- 6 ripe tomatoes
- 1 onion, chop-up
- 3 cloves garlic, chop-up
- 2 tbsp olive oil
- 1 tsp dried basil
- 1 tsp dried oregano
- Salt and pepper as needed
- Fresh basil leaves (for garnish)

Instructions:
1. Turn on the oven to 400 °F (200 °C).
2. On a baking sheet, arrange the tomatoes and red bell peppers. Add salt and pepper and drizzle with olive oil.
3. The peppers and tomatoes Must be roasted in the preheated oven for 20 to 25 mins, or up to their skins begin to blister and turn black.
4. The peppers and tomatoes Must have some time to cool down when you take out the baking sheet from the oven.
5. Peel the skins from the tomatoes and peppers after they have cooled. The peppers Must be seeded.
6. Olive oil Must be heated in a pan over medium heat. Add the chop-up garlic and onion, both chop-up. The onion Must be cooked up to tender and transparent.
7. To the pan, add the roasted peppers and tomatoes. Add the dried oregano and basil.
8. Cook for a short while to enable the flavors to mingle.
9. Blend the Mixture with an immersion blender or in a blender after adding the other ingredients.
10. If necessary, season with more salt and pepper.
11. Serve the hot roasted red pepper and tomato puree with fresh basil leaves as a garnish.

Nutrition (per serving):

Cals: Approximately 90 kcal, Fat: 5g

Carbs: 10g, Fiber: 3g, Protein: 2g

54. MASHED CAULIFLOWER AND CARROT

Prep Time: 15 mins

Cook Time: 20 mins

Total Time: 35 mins

Servings: 4

Ingredients:

- 1 head cauliflower, chop-up into florets
- 2 Big carrots, peel off and chop-up
- 2 cloves garlic, chop-up
- 2 tbsp butter
- 1/4 cup of milk (adjust to preferred consistency)
- Salt and pepper as needed
- Chop-up chives (for garnish)

Instructions:

1. In a pot of boiling water, add the diced carrots and cauliflower florets. Cook for 15 to 20 mins or up to they are tender.
2. Returning the cooked vegetables to the saucepan after draining them.
3. Add the butter and chop-up garlic to the same pot. Using a fork or potato masher, combine the veggies and garlic together.
4. As you mash, gradually add the milk up to the required consistency is reached.
5. To your liking, add salt and pepper to the mashed Mixture.
6. Warm the mashed Mixture through by cooking it for a few mins on low heat.
7. Hot mashed cauliflower and carrots Must be served with chop-up chives as a garnish.

Nutrition (per serving):

Cals: Approximately 90 kcal, Fat: 5g

Carbs: 10g, Fiber: 4g, Protein: 3g

55. BLUEBERRY BANANA COCONUT SMOOTHIE

Prep Time: 5 mins

Total Time: 5 mins

Servings: 2

Ingredients:

- 1 ripe banana
- 1 cup of blueberries (fresh or refrigerated)
- 1/2 cup of coconut milk
- 1/2 cup of Greek yogurt
- 1 tbsp honey (adjust as needed)
- 1/2 tsp vanilla extract

- Ice cubes (non-compulsory)

Instructions:
1. Blend together the banana, blueberries, Greek yogurt, coconut milk, honey, and vanilla extract.
2. Add a few ice cubes for a cooler smoothie if you like.
3. Blend every item up to it is creamy and smooth.
4. If necessary, add more honey after tasting to regulate the sweetness.
5. Serve the smoothie right away after pouring it into glasses.

Nutrition (per serving):

Cals: Approximately 150 kcal, Fat: 6g, Carbs: 23g, Fiber: 3g, Protein: 4g

56. SILKEN TOFU BERRY BREAKFAST SMOOTHIE

Prep Time: 5 mins

Cook Time: 0 mins

Total Time: 5 mins

Servings: 2

Ingredients:
- 1 cup of combined berries (strawberries, blueberries, raspberries)
- 1/2 cup of silken tofu
- 1 ripe banana
- 1/2 cup of almond milk (or any milk of your choice)
- 1 tbsp honey or maple syrup (non-compulsory)
- 1/2 tsp vanilla extract

Instructions:
1. The combined berries, silken tofu, banana, almond milk, honey or maple syrup (if used), and vanilla extract Must all be blended together.
2. Blend up to creamy and smooth on high.
3. Taste, and if necessary, add additional honey or maple syrup to balance sweetness.
4. Pour into glasses and start serving right away.

Nutrition (per serving):

Cals: Approximately 150, Protein: 6g

Carbs: 25g, Fat: 3g, Fiber: 4g

57. CREAMY CARROT AND GINGER SOUP

Prep Time: 10 mins

Cook Time: 25 mins

Total Time: 35 mins

Servings: 4

Ingredients:

- 1 lb carrots, peel off and chop-up
- 1 onion, chop-up
- 2 cloves garlic, chop-up
- 1 tbsp fresh ginger, finely grated
- 4 cups of vegetable broth
- 1 cup of coconut milk
- Salt and pepper as needed
- Fresh cilantro or parsley for garnish

Instructions:

1. Sauté the chop-up garlic and lightly diced onion in a saucepan up to aromatic.
2. Add the finely grated ginger and split carrots. For a few more mins, sauté.
3. The veggie broth Must be added and brought to a boil. Up to the carrots are cooked, lower the heat and let it simmer.
4. Up to the soup is creamy, purée it using an immersion blender.
5. Add the coconut milk, stir, and boil for a further five mins.
6. As needed, add salt and pepper to the food.
7. Hot soup Must be served with fresh parsley or cilantro as a garnish.

Nutrition (per serving):

Cals: Approximately 180, Protein: 2g

Carbs: 15g, Fat: 13g, Fiber: 3g

58. SPINACH AND GREEN PEA PUREE

Prep Time: 5 mins

Cook Time: 10 mins

Total Time: 15 mins

Servings: 3

Ingredients:

- 2 cups of baby spinach
- 1 cup of green peas (fresh or refrigerated)
- 1 tbsp olive oil
- 1 clove garlic, chop-up
- 1/4 tsp cumin
- Salt and pepper as needed
- Squeeze of lemon juice

Instructions:

1. Green peas Must be steamed or boiled up to soft. Drain, then set apart.

2. Heat the olive oil in a pan, then cook the chop-up garlic up to it is fragrant.
3. Sauté the young spinach up to wilted after adding it.
4. In a mixer, combine the cooked green peas, sautéed spinach, cumin, salt, pepper, and a squeeze of lemon juice.
5. Add a little water if necessary to reach the desired consistency and blend up to smooth.
6. If required, taste and adjust the seasoning.
7. Warm the puree before using it as a dip or side dish.

Nutrition (per serving):

Cals: Approximately 80, Protein: 4g, Carbs: 10g, Fat: 3g, Fiber: 4g

59. GREEK YOGURT AND ALMOND PARFAIT

Prep Time: 10 mins

Cook Time: 0 mins

Total Time: 10 mins

Servings: 2

Ingredients:
- 1 cup of Greek yogurt
- 1/2 cup of granola
- 1/4 cup of almonds, chop-up
- 1 cup of combined berries (strawberries, blueberries, raspberries)
- Honey or maple syrup for drizzling (non-compulsory)

Instructions:
1. Place Greek yogurt, granola, almonds, and combined berries in serving glasses or bowls.
2. If desired, drizzle with honey or maple syrup.
3. Depending on the dimensions of your serving dishes, repeat the layers as necessary.
4. Serve right away for a filling and delectable breakfast or snack.

Nutrition (per serving):

Cals: Approximately 300, Protein: 15g

Carbs: 30g, Fat: 15g, Fiber: 6g

60. SOFT SCRAMBLED EGGS WITH SMOKED SALMON:

Prep Time: 5 mins

Cook Time: 5 mins

Total Time: 10 mins

Servings: 2

Ingredients:

- 4 Big eggs
- 1/4 cup of milk or cream
- Salt and pepper as needed
- 2 tbsp butter
- 4 ozs smoked salmon, chop-up
- Chop-up fresh chives for garnish

Instructions:

1. Eggs, milk or cream, salt, and pepper Must all be thoroughly blended in a bowl.
2. Melt the butter in a nonstick skillet over low to medium heat.
3. After pouring the egg Mixture into the skillet, wait a short while before moving on.
4. With a spatula, gently whisk the eggs, moving them from the edges to the middle.
5. The eggs Must continue to boil and whisk up to they are just barely set but not quite set.
6. Shortly whisk in the chop-up smoked salmon to blend and rewarm it.
7. Get rid of the heat. The eggs will continue to be cooked to perfection by the residual heat.
8. Scrambled eggs Must be served with some chop-up chives on top.

NUTRITION INFO:

Cals: ~250 per serving, Protein: ~20g, Fat: ~18g

Carbs: ~2g

61. CREAMY TOMATO AND RED PEPPER BISQUE:

Prep Time: 15 mins

Cook Time: 25 mins

Total Time: 40 mins

Servings: 4

Ingredients:
- 2 tbsp olive oil
- 1 onion, chop-up
- 2 cloves garlic, chop-up
- 2 red bell peppers, roasted, peel off, and chop-up
- 1 can (28 oz) diced tomatoes
- 2 cups of vegetable broth
- 1 tsp dried basil
- 1/2 cup of heavy cream
- Salt and pepper as needed
- Fresh basil leaves for garnish

Instructions:
1. Olive oil Must be heated in a sizable pot over medium heat. When the onion is transparent, add it and continue to cook.
2. Once aromatic, add the chop-up garlic and simmer for one more min.
3. Add the dried basil, diced tomatoes (with juice), vegetable broth, and roasted red peppers. Simmer for a while.
4. To enable the flavors to merge, let the Mixture simmer for 15 to 20 mins.
5. Up to the soup is creamy, purée it using an immersion blender. Alternately, you might add the Mixture in stages to a blender, puree it up to smooth, and then add it back to the saucepan.
6. Add the heavy cream, then simmer the soup for an additional five mins.
7. As needed, add salt and pepper to the food.
8. Serve the bisque hot with fresh basil leaves as a garnish.

NUTRITION INFO:

Cals: ~220 per serving, Protein: ~4g

Fat: ~15g, Carbs: ~20g

62. BANANA PEANUT BUTTER PROTEIN SMOOTHIE:

Prep Time: 5 mins

Cook Time: 0 mins

Total Time: 5 mins

Servings: 2

Ingredients:

- 2 ripe bananas
- 2 tbsp peanut butter
- 1 scoop protein powder (whey or plant-based)
- 1 cup of milk (dairy or plant-based)
- 1/2 cup of Greek yogurt
- 1 tbsp honey (non-compulsory, for sweetness)
- Ice cubes

Instructions:

1. Peel the bananas and slice them roughly.
2. Bananas that have been slice, peanut butter, protein powder, milk, Greek yogurt, and honey (if using) Must all be combined in a blender.
3. A few ice cubes Must be added to the combiner.
4. Blend at a high speed just up to the Mixture becomes creamy and smooth.
5. You can add more milk to the smoothie if it is too thick to get the consistency you want.
6. Serve the smoothie right away after pouring it into glasses.

NUTRITION INFO:

Cals: ~300 per serving, Protein: ~15g

Fat: ~10g, Carbs: ~40g

Made in United States
Troutdale, OR
04/15/2025